Mick Digs

Written by Caroline Green

Illustrated by Lucy Barnard

Collins

Mick digs pits

Kit picks pots

Mick digs pits

Kit picks pots

Mick pops in pips

sacks

Mick pops in pips

sacks

Kit tips

cat

Kit tips

cat

/c/

14

/g/

☙ Review: After reading ☙

Use your assessment from hearing the children read to choose any GPCs or words that need additional practice.

Read 1: Decoding

- Ensure the children can read words ending in "s" successfully. Ask the children to turn to pages 2–3. Show them how to read the word **digs** by covering up the "s", reading the word "dig" and then adding the "s" to read the whole word **digs**.

- Turn to page 4. Ask the children to read the words. Ask: Which word contains the sound /g/? (**digs**)

- Look at pages 9 to 11 and challenge the children to find three different spellings of the same sound /c/. (**sacks**, *ck*; **Kit**, *k*; **cat**, *c*)

- Look at the "I spy sounds" pages (14–15) together. How many objects can the children point to that contain the /c/ sound and the /g/ sound? (e.g. *kingfisher, beak, kite, cat, key, ketchup, drink, cricket/ grasshopper, rocks*; *grapes, bug, glass, grass, gloves, golf club/balls, greenhouse, garden*)

Read 2: Vocabulary

- Go back through the book and discuss the pictures. Encourage children to talk about details that stand out for them. Use a dialogic talk model to expand on their ideas and recast them in full sentences as naturally as possible.

- Work together to expand vocabulary by naming objects in the pictures that children do not know.

- Turn to pages 8 and 9. Ask: Which word means "puts"? (**pops**) Point to **sacks**. Ask: Can you think of another word for "sacks"? (e.g. *bags, packs*)

Read 3: Comprehension

- Turn to pages 4 and 5. Ask the children: Why do you think Mick is digging? (e.g. *to make holes to put the seeds in*; *to plant the seeds*)

- Turn to pages 10 and 11. Ask: What does Kit tip? (*a watering can*) Why does she do this? (*to water the seeds*)

- Ask the children what they think will happen next (e.g. *the seeds will begin to grow and plants will appear*)

- Ask the children: Have you ever planted any seeds? What did you plant? Where? What happened?